Yes, You Can't!

The Power of  Thinking

Ruth Cullen

 PETER PAUPER PRESS, INC.
WHITE PLAINS, NEW YORK

Why have AMBITION when you can just lower the bar?

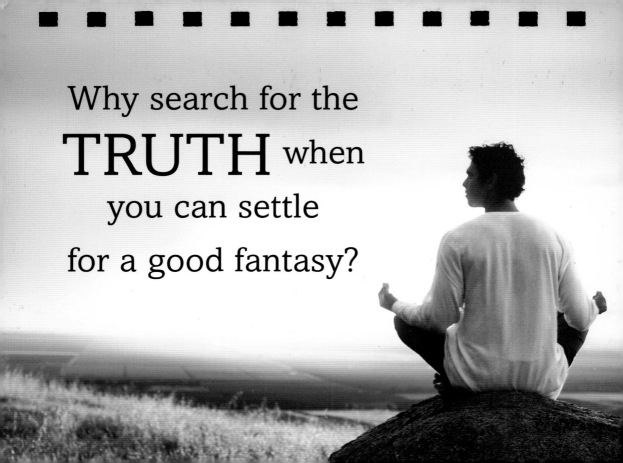

COURAGE is doing what you're afraid to do.

INTELLIGENCE is getting someone else to do it.

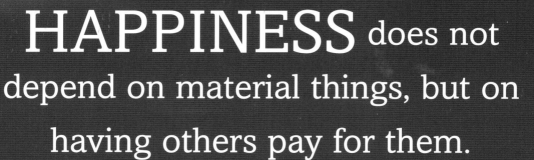

HAPPINESS does not depend on material things, but on having others pay for them.

INNER PEACE
is achieved only after you surrender
all notions that excellence
is within your reach.

LOYALTY means wearing the company golf shirt after your job has been shipped overseas.

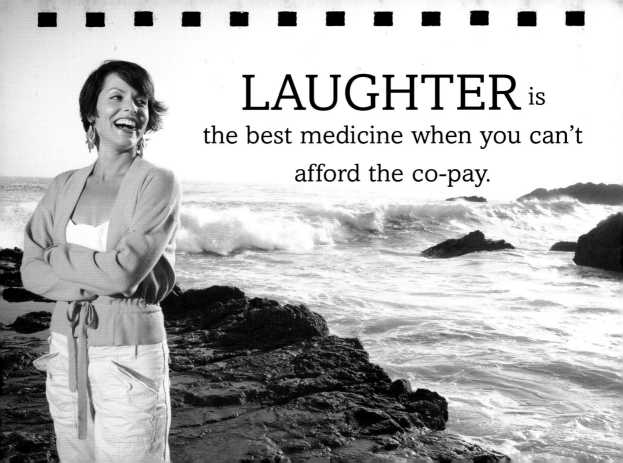

LAUGHTER is the best medicine when you can't afford the co-pay.

KNOWLEDGE

may have its limits, but

ignorance knows no bounds.

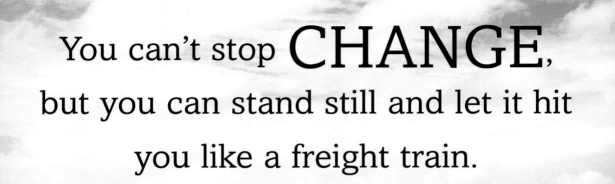

You can't stop CHANGE, but you can stand still and let it hit you like a freight train.

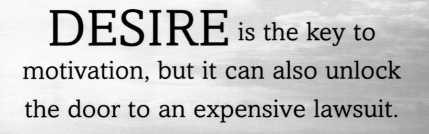

DESIRE is the key to motivation, but it can also unlock the door to an expensive lawsuit.

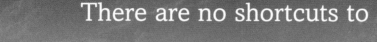

There are no shortcuts to

ACHIEVEMENT,

but it never hurts to look.

If ignorance is BLISS, the bird of happiness must visit you often.

Today is a PRESENT
and tomorrow a gift,
thanks to yesterday's credit cards.

True FAMILY members are the ones who understand the magnitude of your failures and never let you forget them.

MARRIAGE

is the foundation

upon which

all great fights

are built.

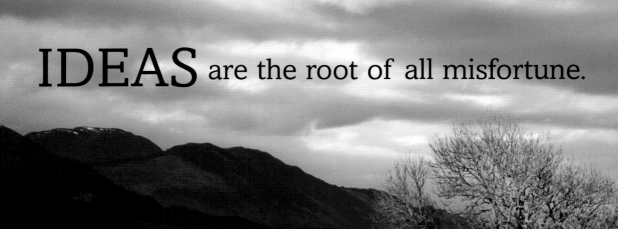

IDEAS are the root of all misfortune.

Why aspire to **GREATNESS** when mediocrity pays just as well?

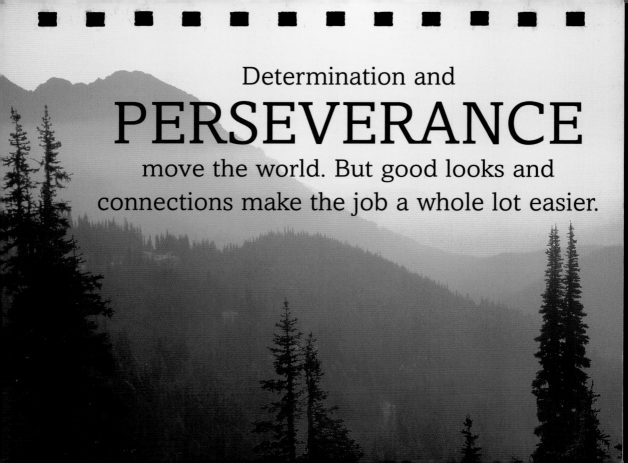

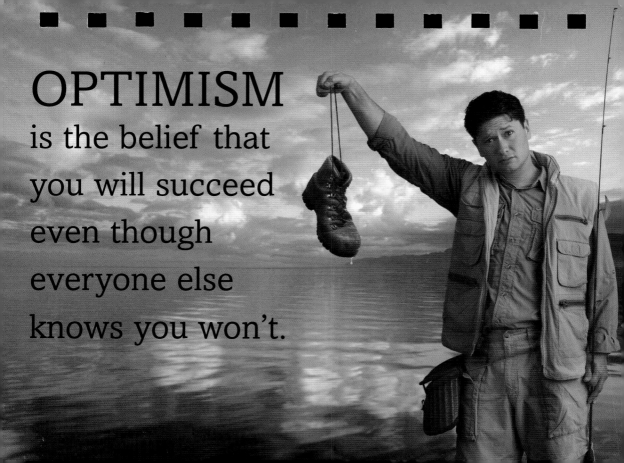

When in doubt, always trust your INTUITION to make the right decision.

Because your intuition is never wrong, right?

PATIENCE is a virtue, but laziness disguised as patience is a skill.

ACCEPTANCE

means embracing the fact
that your greatest weakness
is having no strengths.

FRIENDSHIP with oneself is all-important, especially when you have no other friends.

UNDERSTANDING

the depth of your inadequacy

is the first step to covering it up.

Follow your PASSION to the ends of the earth but don't stalk it, lest you get slapped with a restraining order.

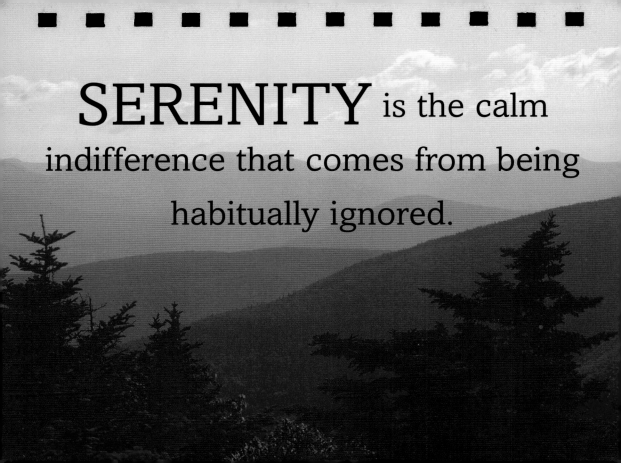

You are never too old to set new

GOALS, but you can be

too old to remember them.

Weep not that the world changes

over TIME,

but that you

remain stagnant.

May you have the hindsight to know where you've been, the foresight to know where you're going, and the INSIGHT to get a good lawyer.

In **NATURE**, a weed is just a flower in disguise.

In the workplace, a weed is just a weed, until it is promoted into management.

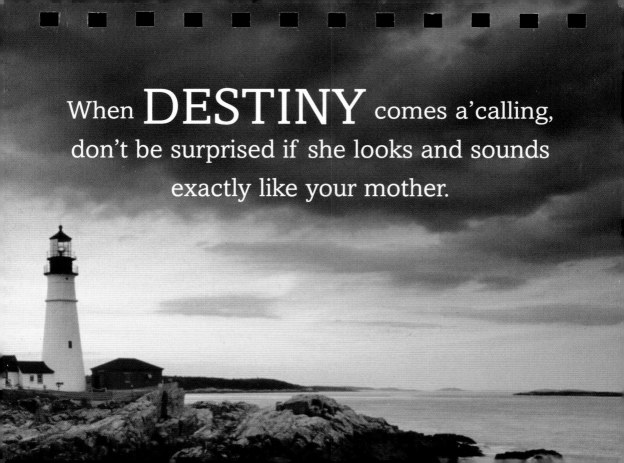

When DESTINY comes a'calling, don't be surprised if she looks and sounds exactly like your mother.

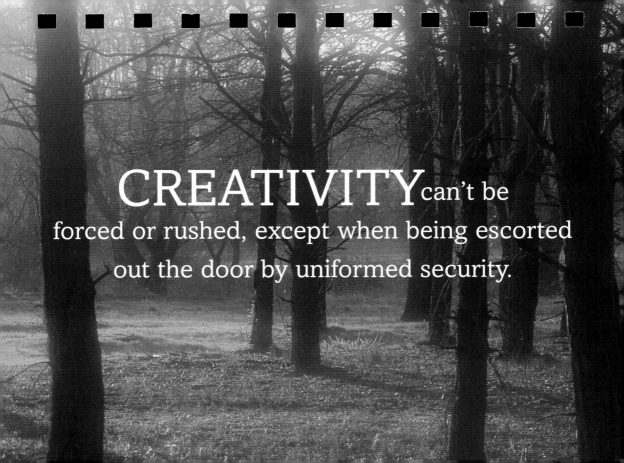

Use what TALENT you possess—if only to make everyone else feel better about themselves.

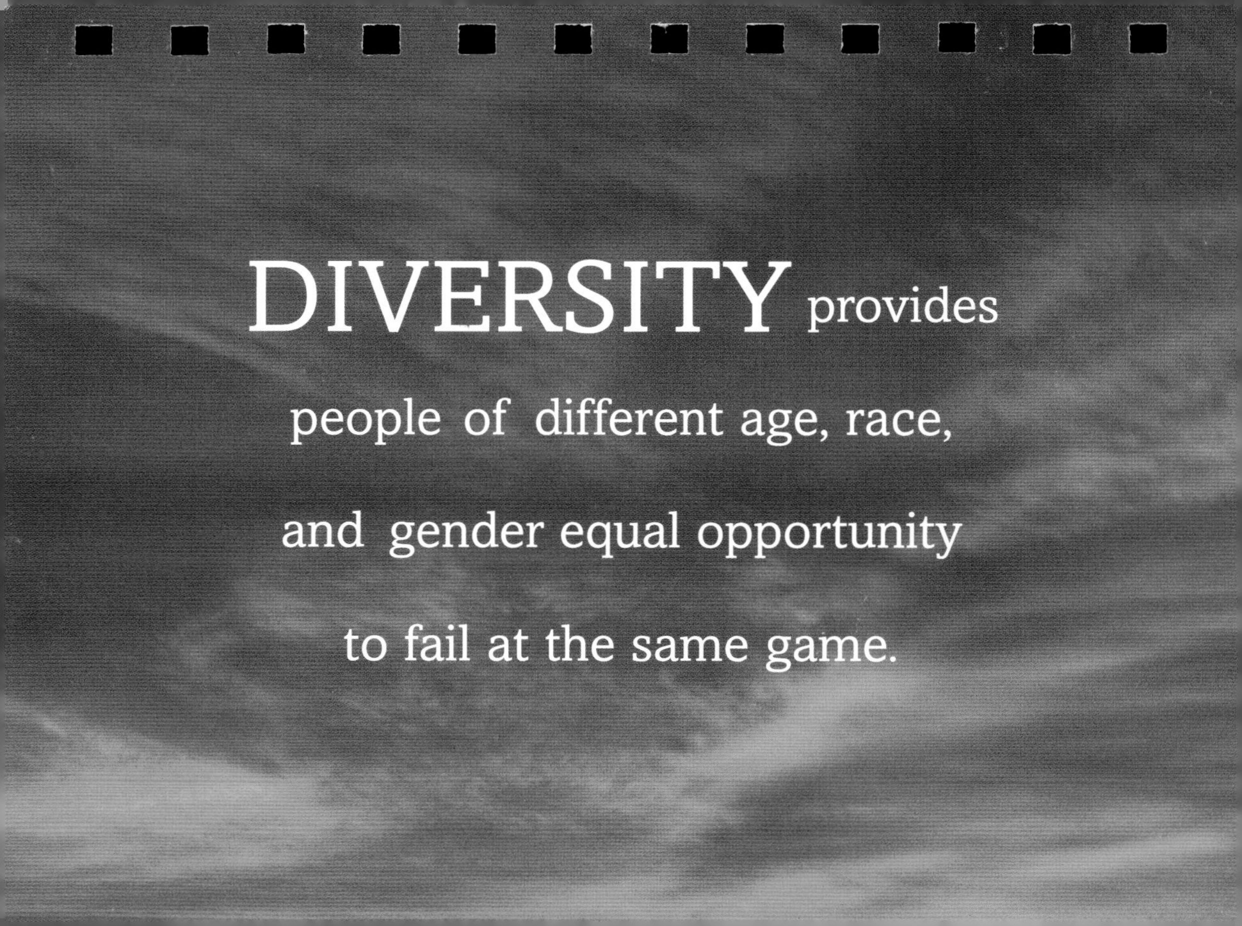
DIVERSITY provides
people of different age, race,
and gender equal opportunity
to fail at the same game.

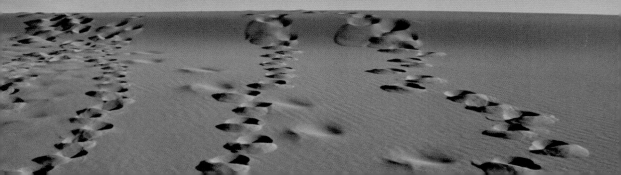

FAITH is believing
that a small group of thoughtful,
committed citizens can do anything at all.

A life of PROSPERITY is within your reach, but snatching it can carry a sentence of about 15 to 20.

If you dare to believe in
the beauty of your DREAMS,
just remember:
beauty is only skin deep.

Never underestimate the POWER of a fancy title and some shiny shoes.

HONESTY is always the best policy when required by law.

CONFIDENCE

is the feeling you have

before you understand

the situation.

Life isn't about WINNING or losing.
At least, that's what the losers say.